# TEACH US TO PRAY

# Teach Us To Pray

## AN ANCIENT MODEL FOR A MODERN DAY

Rev. Melissa Ebken

Melissa Ebken, Light Life and Love Ministries

# Contents

*This book is for all the saints
that have mentored me in this
journey of faith.*

# Reviews

Refreshing! Rev. Melissa Ebken brings a wide-eyed look at the prayer Jesus taught his followers when they asked him, "how should we pray?" We are reminded that this prayer which has been memorized by countless followers of Jesus and recited with care in worship ritual, has the power to bring light back into the eyes of a patient with Alzheimer dementia.

It also has the capacity to aid newcomers in faith as they try to understand the nature of following in Jesus' foot-steps, and the world he prayed for---"thy Kingdom come." Rev. Ebken writes as someone who knows what it means to be new to something and struggling to find your way. It is not with a specific proscription---this is how it is. Instead, she invites her listeners to join in the journey. She asks only that we "come and see."

And, to those who need a fresh look at what they have been praying for years, she opens the possibility of new insight, learning and deepening. Phrase by phrase, we are invited to hear and see what we have been praying---and what that might mean for the life of our world.

The book is structured as an essay with reflection ques-tions at the end of each chapter based on one phrase of the prayer. The essays are a window into the phrase, and the author's joyful soul. Alone as a journal of discovery, or in a group who want to deepen their prayer life, Rev. Ebken lights a way. *-Rev. Dr. Teresa Dulyea-Parker, Regional Minis-*

ter and President of the Christian Church in Illinois and Wisconsin

Our most basic understanding of prayer is as a lopsided conversation with God. An opportunity to show our gratitude, make a request, or simply meditate, but prayer is a profoundly important experience for people of faith. However, despite its importance, many of us have never given it proper consideration. Perhaps we feel that, as a deeply personal and private matter, prayer defies critical scrutiny. But a more meaningful consideration of how and why we pray offers opportunities to enhance our faith and enrich our lives.

In *The Lord's Prayer: An Old Model for a Modern Day*, Melissa Ebken, a seminary-trained pastor at a Christian church in Central Illinois, has given us a modern-day primer for prayer based on both biblical scholarship and her own personal experiences with faith and prayer. Beginning with her earliest experiences with prayer, Ebken takes us on a journey that spans the Old and New Testaments of the Bible and her years of experience in ministry. Throughout the book, Ebken displays a seasoned pastor's knack for making difficult theological concepts accessible to laypeople.

In order to make it easier for the reader to apply the lessons and concepts taught in the book, there are questions at the end of each chapter. The book is based on a series of sermons that Ebken presented to her church congregation.

The Lord's Prayer serves as the central theme of the book, and specific passages are used as topics for the individual chapters. The book explores the deeper meaning and relevance of each passage, but they also serve as a jumping off point for discussions about different aspects of prayer and faith. The concept is well executed by the author, and throughout the book she writes in a style that is both erudite and conversational.

But what I most admired and appreciated about this book was the author's ability to relate these lessons without judgement or condescension. For example, she points out that praying for favors from God is probably a questionable practice, but admits that she's done the same thing herself. She makes a similar confession about her struggles with forgiveness in a later chapter. Instead of scolding the reader for selfish prayer habits or morally questionable behavior, she points to scripture and her own personal experiences to identify opportunities for greater spiritual fulfillment through prayer and faith.

Ultimately, this book does an outstanding job of giving us what we most want from such books: food for our spiritual souls. The book is uplifting and inspirational. It provides a pleasant escape from our daily tedium and allows us to contemplate the wonders of our creator. No, as she reminds us in the third chapter, God will not give us everything we want, but, if we put our faith in Him, He will provide us with everything we need. And that is enough.
-*Mike Warren, Entrepreneur*

# 1

# How Do We Pray?

**Introduction**

*"Pray then in this way:*
*Our Father in heaven,*
*hallowed be your name.*
*Your kingdom come.*
*Your will be done,*
*on earth as it is in heaven.*
*Give us this day our daily bread.*
*And forgive us our debts,*
*as we also have forgiven our debtors.*

*And do not bring us to the time of trial,*
*but rescue us from the evil one."*
*Matthew 6:9-13 NRSV*

When I was a child, I felt like it was important to pray before bedtime. I didn't have any instruction on this, so I did the best I could. I knew two prayers: the 'Now I lay me down to sleep' prayer and the Lord's prayer. Each night I would say these, in this order. The order felt important to me, although I'm not sure why. These two prayers sustained me throughout my childhood, even into adulthood. Whenever I have no words, I still have these. These prayers bring me back to that simple, centered place where I remember who and Whose I am.

When I got all grown up (became a teenager) I felt like I should pray in a more grown-up way. I began establishing a pattern of prayer that went something like this: 'Hi God I love you and thanks for everything, here's what I want, here's what I'm willing to do for it, and here's the timeframe I'm looking at. In Jesus' name, Amen.' I'm embarrassed to say how long that pattern formed my prayers. God did a LOT of heavy lifting growing my spirit.

Later, I was called into ministry (absolutely not one of my prayer requests) and realized that I needed to do some work in the area of prayer. If God wanted me to be a spiritual leader of actual people (seriously, God?) then I needed deeper roots. The only way I knew to do that was to deepen my understanding of prayer. I figured I would turn to the source. Jesus taught the disciples a model for prayer, because, apparently, it's not intuitive for most of us.

I had been praying the Lord's Prayer daily for most of my life. I realized that Jesus gave them a *model* for prayer. Repeating that model had kept me nearer to God in my life, so leaning into that model, in itself, was a life-giving practice.

Once, I was given reassurance of that when I did a nursing home visit with my pastor. We visited a man who had advanced Alzheimer's disease. When we spoke, he showed no understanding, no cognition even, that we were speaking to him. However, when my pastor began praying the Lord's Prayer, his back straightened, and he began to pray along with her. Word for word. I was frozen in awe as I understood what was happening in front of me. This man had prayed these words so many times throughout his life that they had become written on his heart. Beyond all consciousness, beyond all sense of decision or recognition, he knew the words that connected him to God. It's a lesson I haven't forgotten.

Yes, repeating the model of prayer that Jesus gave the disciples has real value. If we pray no other words, that will keep us nearer to the heart of God.

But there's more.

When we take these words as a model for prayer, we will see doors opened for us in ways we haven't previously experienced. In fact, I would go so far to say that this model for prayer forms us as disciples and propels us as agents of wholeness and reconciliation in our world.

We first read of this model for prayer in Matthew, tucked into the Sermon on The Mount. We encounter it again in Luke, when one of the disciples asks Jesus to teach them how to pray. In this book, I am using the model Jesus gave in Matthew 6 in the Sermon on The Mount. My purpose is to open for you the power of this model for prayer that has made God real to me, and has propelled me to great depths of faith.

This book is adapted from a sermon series I did over five weeks. Each chapter will address an aspect of this prayer model, followed by questions that allow you to go deeper in your own faith life. May God bless your journey.

# 2

# What Is God's Name?



*Scripture: Pray then in this way: Our Father in heaven hallowed be your name*

Have you ever wondered how to pray, or how to pray more effectively? Is there a special way I should be praying? Jesus addresses this. Taken from the Sermon on the Mount in Matthew, he says that when you are praying, "do not heap up empty phrases as the Gentiles do, for they think they will be heard because of their many words. Do not be like them for your Father knows what you need, even before you ask him. Pray then in this way."

Let's look at the first sentence: "Our Father in heaven, hallowed be thy name." So, when we talk about praying, the first thing to address, is how we address God. How do we come before God and what do we call God?

We first hear of God's name back in Exodus, when Moses is called to the burning bush. He's minding his own business, taking care of his father in-law's sheep. Out of nowhere, a scrubby bush begins to glow with fire, but it isn't being consumed. He's never seen anything like it before! And from this on-fire-but-not burning- bush, he hears a voice calling him nearer. There doesn't seem to be anyone else around. The sheep are not disturbed, in fact they are quite at peace. The air still smells like sheep, not burning wood, and yet, there – right in front of him – is this presence…. A voice calls out to Moses and tells him to take off his shoes and step forward; he is on holy ground. "Who is this who calls me by name and speaks from this odd fire-but-not-quite-a-fire?"

As Moses stepped onto the holy ground, The Voice called out to him and told him to go back to Egypt (where he headed the 10 most wanted list by the way) and walk up to Pharaoh (chief enforcer of the most wanted list) and demand that Pharaoh allow Moses' fellow Hebrews to be released from their four-hundred-year slavery so they may go out across the land and praise their God. But there's a burning question tugging at Moses.

"Who are you? Who are you that you would bring me here, who are you that you would send me back to the place from which I fled to save my neck? Who are you to send someone like me, who doesn't even speak well, to waltz into the heavily fortified palace and make such a demand of the most powerful human on earth? Who are you…?"

That's a good question, don't you think? Once we know someone's name, we know something about who he or she is. Who is The Voice and by what authority does it ask such a thing of Moses? Not to mention, when (if) he gets in front of the most powerful person on earth and delivers a proclamation that will upend Pharaoh's economy, who shall he say sent him? He's going to need a little more than some guy in a bush. Moses has no idea that the answer to his query will change his entire understanding of how life is ordered.

"I AM," says the voice.

…What's that now?

"I AM." The One who speaks from the bush is known as the One who is, who was, who always shall be. The One who is called I AM is The One who is present and creating in every moment. Someone named I AM is a pretty big deal. Probably a bigger deal than Pharaoh.

Those words, spoken in Hebrew, mean I Am. It is an ongoing sense, it is not merely I Was, or I Will Be. It is both of those things and it is I AM. I AM! This encompassed all that God was, all that God is, and all that God will be. That tense there, AM, implies an ongoing thing. Are you creating something? I am. That means there has been an action, there is an action, and there will continue to be an action.

That name was such an important part of the ancient Hebrews' understanding of God, that they did not say it out loud! Out of respect and reverence to God, that name was not uttered. They would call God Adonai, or Elohim, words that mean Lord Almighty, or Mighty God. But never, never would they address God directly by name.

When you had that as your understanding of who God is, what kind of God does that represent for you? Does that represent a personal God? Or, maybe a more distant yet powerful God? A God that is not so easily accessible. This is the God of their tradition. This is the God of hundreds of years, of generation after generation after generation; the great I AM! The Name that would never be uttered except for one day a year, the day of atonement, the holiest of holy days in the temple. The high priest, one time, once a year, would address God as I Am. There was an air of reverence. How does one dare to approach I AM in prayer? Is it just better to leave that to the professionals?

That's where the disciples and other folks were in their faith. So, they come to Jesus – are drawn to him – and he is about to reveal to them how they, themselves, can approach I AM.

"Well," Jesus said, "I call God, Abba." I call God Abba. Now 'Ab' is father, 'Abba' is the more familiar or intimate form of Father, which would be equal to our 'Daddy.' WHAT? So, could you imagine, sitting there as a disciple and Jesus saying, when you pray, pray like this: "Daddy in heaven." They probably didn't hear anything after that point. Because this is the one who they addressed without even using the actual words of his/her name. That name is holy and is only spoken by one person, one time a year, and here is Jesus saying call God, Daddy! Can you imagine?

That changes how you would view God, doesn't it? The I AM is a big, almighty, powerful, up in the heavens, thunder and lightning, God of the mountains, God! To call God "Daddy?" That brings God to a different level of perspective altogether, doesn't it? Well, maybe it doesn't bring God to a different perspective, but it brings us into a different relationship with God. That starkly changed their understanding of who God was.

What do you call God when you pray? In church we often address God as Gracious and Loving God, Father, (we're still rather blown away by the thought of using the way too familiar Daddy) or by adjectives such as gracious, loving, compassionate, or almighty. Have you ever expanded what you call God? I never had. I was challenged by my pastor years ago to address God as something different every time I prayed for two weeks. I said "Ok, whatever" (probably rolled my eyes)! Would you believe it profoundly changed my relationship with and understanding of God? PROFOUNDLY!

It doesn't seem like that big of a deal, but I am

telling you, it is. I think one of the reasons why is that it makes you stop and think of what you need in the moment. There were times when I was driving my car and there was an awful snowstorm, a blizzard, I couldn't see two feet in front of me and I needed God, My Father, to come down and stop it and make everything be ok, to fix what was broken. There were times as a new mother that I wanted My Mom. At three in the morning I needed Mother God to radiate the confidence and wisdom of generations of women. There have been times when I prayed that I felt like I wanted to crawl into my grandmother's lap and just curl up there, and be rocked, and comforted. To be able to address God in that fashion brought me to a different place. There are times when I want that God of the mountains, I want the almighty, powerful God. There are times when I am that lost sheep on the back side of the mountain, and I want that searching God, that God of the prodigal.

When I address God, I now stop and think about where I am in my journey, what I need from God, and it doesn't change who God is, but it makes it clearer to me my place with God. God is I

AM, always was, always will be. God is all of these things. And so much more.

There are times when you go to your best friend and need that friend to hold you accountable, you need that from your friend. There are times when you go to that same friend and you need a shoulder to cry on, and there are times when you go to that friend because you feel silly and want someone else to be silly with you. Your best friend is all of those things, but we approach each other differently depending on our needs and our circumstances at the time. What does it say about us and our understanding of God that we call upon God in these different and varied postures?

It means we can be fully ourselves with God. There is no need to clean up first. How does that change your faith to know that you can be absolutely, authentically yourself in the presence of God, and God will embrace you as you are?

I pass on to you the challenge that was given to me: when you pray, stop for a minute, how are you going to address God? Address God in a different way than you have before. I promise you, it will affect your relationship and understanding of God!

Jesus knew this too, that is why he gave them that example. In the gospel of John, Jesus tells us many other things. Jesus has 7 I am statements in the gospel of John:

"I AM the bread of life," for those of you who are hungry, I am what you are looking for.

"I Am the light of the world," those who are living in darkness and need help, need promise, and need a brighter way tomorrow, I AM that light.

"I AM the door of the sheep," if you need to find a Savior I AM the doorway, the path to what you seek.

"I AM the Good Shepherd." I am that person who will lead you, will guide you, call you home, and search for you.

"I AM the Resurrection and the Life." I AM a living, breathing live entity among you, and will make you just as I AM.

"I AM the way, the truth, and the light," Jesus said. Do you want to know who God is? Here is the way. Do you want to know what God's words are to you today? Here's the truth. Do you want to know how to stand in the kingdom of God, now and forever? I am the life, Jesus says.

Do you need a little bit of discipline, do you need to work on obedience? "I AM the Vine," Jesus says. When Jesus says I AM, it is on purpose and a direct reference back to who God is, to who God disclosed to humanity that s/he is. I AM.

So, how do we pray? Well, the first thing to consider is, take a breath, where are you in this moment? Relate to God honestly, intimately, because God is all of these things. What do you need? "I AM", God says.

I promise you, your relationship with God will open up in a new, exciting way when you address God in these different ways, because in doing so, you will realize that God is The One who is All.

That is a foundation one can build upon.

Thanks be to God, who wants to be known. Amen

### For Further Reflection

1. What do you call God? What does this imply about how you relate to/understand God?

2. When was a time you needed God in a way that was different from your traditional understanding?

3. What changes for you when you call God in the way you need God?

4. How might this practice affect how faith communities form?

5. How might this affect the way we share God with others?

3

# What Does God Want?

*Thy kingdom come, thy will be done, on earth as it is in heaven.*

I don't recall ever having a Sunday school class that taught me how to pray. I guess, like most of us, it's something I've put together on my own. I often have found that throughout my life my prayers have been pretty prescriptive, going something like this: "Okay God, here's what I want, here's the time frame I'm looking at, and these are the boundaries in which I'm willing to participate." Does this sound familiar?

And then we go about our business and look

for God to pull that together for us. We love God, we love Jesus, we do our best to be nice to people (even the really annoying ones) so we should get this, right? Don't we deserve it for being so patient and tolerant? A day might pass, or a week, and we're looking around for the curtain to draw back and the answer to our prayers to present itself. Maybe we wait a tad longer…

Then we get impatient. We get frustrated. What's the deal, God? Where's the answer to that prayer? You know I read an extra page of my Bible every day last week, right?

All of us have had experiences when our prayers seemed to go unanswered; sometimes days, weeks, months, or even years will go by at a time and we still find ourselves wondering, "God when are you going to answer my prayer?" It has been a minute since I prayed, why am I not seeing any results yet? It's hard to remember that God hasn't forgotten us, nor abandoned us. The Bible tells us that God goes before us and will be with us. God will never leave or forsake us. Do not be afraid. Do not be discouraged. God has promised to answer every prayer, according to God's grace and power. God is able to do immeasurably more than all we ask or even imagine.

The line of prayer says, thy kingdom come, thy will be done. "Oh God, may your kingdom, may your will be a reality on this earth just like it is in heaven." That is a pretty stout prayer and we have been praying that prayer for a long time, not just us, but Christians for thousands of years. We don't yet fully see that prayer realized.

Why not?

What happens with unanswered prayer?

…Is there such a thing?

If we pray "thy will be done" there's no such thing as unanswered prayer. Maybe. Is there?

I imagine someday getting an opportunity to have a conversation (interrogation) with God that goes something like this: God – why haven't you given us peace? Why do so many people live in squalor? Why are so many people hungry, and children victimized, and the powerful getting what they want at the ruin of the powerless? Why, God, do we have to *work* to stop human trafficking? Why, God, do bad things happen to good people? Why does evil thrive and get all the good stuff while righteousness suffers? WHY AREN'T YOU FIXING THIS?

Every time I get to this point in this imagined conversation, I feel the same response from God: I've been wondering the same thing. So many people come to me in prayer wanting a better world; a world that is just and kind and loving. So many prayers come to me pleading for mercy and guidance. So many prayers come to me seeking reconciliation and peace. I've given them every gift they need – time and again – to reconcile all these things. I've given everything I have – even my own self – to humankind. I've been wondering the same thing. WHY AREN'T YOU FIXING THIS?

*crickets*

*crickets*

*crickets*

What's that now?

God: as long as I want this more than you do, nothing will change.

Me: but God, of course I want this, I'm praying for it aren't I?

God: Yes, you are. And in response, I have given you much. I'm waiting for you to put it all to use. Not just you – but all the people who send these prayers. I have provided strength and courage and understanding. Remember all that difficulty you had a while back? Coming through that equipped you for what you now ask. You have what you need, and I AM with you.

*Sigh*

No matter how I come at this, I end up here. And I can see the truth in it. As a parent, I often yearn for my child to rise up and seize an opportunity or realize potential that's his for the taking. I see him waver and I tell him, "You can do this! I know you can! I believe in you – you are stronger than you think!" Ultimately, the choice lies within him. He has to want it more. When he does, he will succeed in ways he never knew possible. He only must decide to do the hard work.

To be honest with you – I would like to come to a different conclusion. I would like for God to be more like Amazon, and my faith to be like a Prime membership, and whatever I pray for would materialize within 2 days. Or soon thereafter (not everything is available with Prime). I would like it if God were like Santa Claus and saw that I was doing well and asked me what I would like to have (I could even live with the naughty list notification and would take the opportunity to rectify that). I would like to pray and know that I could have what I asked for and let God do the heavy lifting and fix the things that are wrong (as I see them) in the world, and please, oh please, let the Cubs win another World Series (that was fun)!

Unfortunately, when I think about God being like this, I see the world in which I already live; this world from which I seek deliverance. If God were merely what *I wanted* God to be, there would be no hope for a better world, because none of us would be able to grow in ways that matter. God would care about the things I care about and do a lot of eye rolling at other stuff. For God to be God, God must be bigger than my image.

I have long known that if I pray for patience, God is going to give me an opportunity to grow my patience. If I ask for humility, God will give me an opportunity to be humbled. If I pray for joy, God will give me the opportunity to recognize the joy around me. If I pray for understanding, God will give me something to understand.

I don't say this to imply that God is capricious, or that God looks for an excuse to make us suffer. I say this to mean that patience and humility and joy and understanding come after the hard work of choosing those things, when it's so much easier and tempting to succumb to the opposites. I become patient when I choose patience over impatience. I become humble when I choose humility. I become joyful when I choose to find and see joy. I understand when I choose to understand.

*Thy kingdom come, thy will be done, on earth as it is in heaven.*

Jesus was giving them a model for prayer. Jesus was telling them to pray in a way that seeks to bring about our own transformation (conversion). Jesus was very clear and upfront about the difficulty of being a disciple. He never once hinted that following him would be easy. In fact, he was clear that it could very well cost us our lives, and would at the very least, make us darned uncomfortable and probably not popular. Choosing to follow Jesus is to choose to do the hard stuff: choosing love, joy, peace, patience, kindness, goodness, faithfulness, generosity, humility, forgiveness, self-control. Choosing Jesus means choosing what matters to God over what feels good and easy and fun for ourselves, for the sake of the world. It means we love other people and want for them every bit of goodness that we want for ourselves. And knowing that that only happens when we do the hard work within ourselves and encourage others as they do the same. It's going to get worse before it gets better. But it gets better. So much better.

*Thy kingdom come, thy will be done, on earth as it is in heaven.*

The really good things in life are worth the hard work. The people with whom you share life, those whom you love and know the most, it's with those people that we can learn and become all of those things that being a disciple requires. We have the place to learn forgiveness and grace, patience and understanding, joy and peace.

Bringing about God's will and God's kingdom begins inside of us, with the choice to do the work. It's honed within our circles of people. Our families, friends, and coworkers are the laboratory where we practice and perfect love. And then it spreads outward. Do you want to change the world? Do you want God to be known and praised by everyone who has breath? Then choose for that to be. Practice these behaviors in your circle of people. Pray as Jesus taught us. Do the hard work. It starts inside of us and is powered by the desire for God's kingdom to come, God's will to be done, on earth as it is in heaven.

When we seek first the kingdom of God, everything else will fall into place. It won't always be easy, it won't always be fun, but it will be to the glory of God, and ultimately, bring all of us to a place of profound joy. Profound love. Profound peace. Because when there is despair, God brings hope. When there is death, God brings new life. God gets the final word, and that word is Life. Now and forever, thy kingdom come, thy will be done, always, absolutely. Amen.

## For Further Reflection

1. How has God brought opportunities to you to grow? Often these come through the most difficult and painful times in our lives. Are you able to see God within and beyond your grief and suffering?
2. What do you envision God's will to be?
3. What motivates you to want to do the hard work of transformation?
4. What waits for you to be transformed once you do the hard work? Who are your

biggest cheerleaders? For whom are you a
cheerleader?

# 4

# What Do We Need?

*Give us this day our daily bread.*

When we talk about our daily bread, it's a reference to ancient times. God's people – the Hebrews – had been enslaved in Egypt for 400 years. Through Moses' leadership and God's power, the Hebrews were able to leave their slavery. Settlement did not happen quickly, though. For forty years they followed where God led them, circling in the wilderness, until they reached the land they had been promised. Each day, as they wandered, God provided manna for them, (bread-like food that appeared on the ground each morning) and only enough for that day, except on the Sabbath (the seventh day of each week and a day of rest and worship). On the Sabbath day, they had a portion from the double portion given the previous day. So, each day God provided what they needed. They always wanted more to store up, but God gave them what they needed.

Now here is the thing: a lot of them wanted something other than manna. When I hear God say, "Hey, I'll be sending you food each day," I think, "I would like my steaks medium and my shrimp with warm garlic butter." That's what I think of when I hear that story. They wanted some surf and turf, but God provided them bologna sandwiches.

Another aspect of that story was that they needed to learn to trust and depend upon God. It was a lesson about knowing the difference between our needs and our wants (such lessons make me scrunch my nose). I would much rather talk about what I want, rather than what I need. I don't like to have to distinguish between the two, but it is important that we do. When we pray, it's helpful to know the difference between need and want, and to pray each day for God to give us what we *need.*

When we talk about needs, there are physical needs: food, shelter, and clothing, we need those each day. We have certain needs for our mental health, as well: a good understanding of ourselves, good boundaries to know who we are and who we are not, and we need healthy relationships.

We also have spiritual needs. If you have been feeling just a little off, lately, or a little restless, maybe it is your soul saying that it needs something. I think there are some basic needs for our souls. First, and foremost, our souls need a foundation. Something true upon which to be rooted, and to stand. My understanding of that has grown and evolved, as I have grown and evolved. It's probably true of you, also.

When I was a child, my "daily bread" was my parents, my brothers, and my family, including my extended family. That was my foundation. Within my family I learned all the basics of life. Those relationships taught me to know right from wrong, held me accountable, how to honor my instincts and emotions, how to think and plan (mostly plot revenge against my older brothers), and how to value all people and life as made in the image of God.

As I got older, I realized that life was slippery and to have a foundation is to have something that isn't temporary or subject to failing, and that God is a better foundation than even my beloved family or anything I could manufacture myself. Maybe the only foundation. I was pretty sure that God was my solid foundation.

When I was on a mission trip in Central America, we had an earthquake come through. I admit it revealed to me that I had assumed that the ground that I stood upon was a solid foundation. All of these rumblings kept coming through, we were out in the middle of nowhere, and if there was any radio reception, sketchy as it was, guess what? It was in Spanish, not English, so we didn't know what was going on. To be honest, the people broadcasting didn't know what was going on either because it was an earthquake, and who knows? We knew that every hour or so, something came through and everything shook, and pitched and we wondered, "Is this the pre-shock, the main event, or an aftershock?"

An hour later another one came. I never contemplated how I depended upon the ground beneath my feet as being a solid foundation. It seems silly, I know, but when the ground laid out in a field before you, looks like a carpet that someone is shaking the dust off of, it can really throw you off for a little bit. At least it did me, I didn't know what was true and what was false, because the ground is supposed to be the ground, it is not supposed to be a wave. The earth's crust is made up of rock and all of these things, it is not supposed to move, but it turns out that it does. So, I needed something more to be a solid foundation, because even the earth beneath my feet can sometimes shake and tremble. And boogie.

Often, in talking with folks, the crises in our lives reveal what we have chosen, either consciously or unconsciously, as a foundation in our lives. Sometimes we have placed our vocation, or our marriage, or our place in society as our foundation. All of that can change in a second. Some have been rocked to the core when the marriage, which had been their foundation, crumbles. Or kids who grow up and no longer need us the way we want them to, or families who move away, or all of these things, they are wonderful, but folks -

they will not be a foundation, and it is unfair to place anyone in the position of being your foundation.

The only foundation that is sure and lasting and deserving of that trust, and that can handle and stand up to being that, is God. What do you say is your everything? If God is not the first thing that comes to mind, then your soul might be trying to tell you something. You might be feeling a little off balance, maybe that is the place to start.

The second need our soul has is for connection, not only to God but to each other. We need that connection to something bigger than all of us. We need a connection to something that transcends this life, and all of our understanding of this life, so that when the earth shakes or when those walls crumble, or whenever all of the things around us that used to be constant are chaotic, we know that there is something beyond all of that. We need that connection to God. Not just the knowledge that God exists, but that deep and abiding connection to God. I'll say a little more about that in a moment.

We also need connection and intimacy with other people. We need people, maybe not a lot of people, maybe just a person. We need someone to keep us oriented. Someone who knows us, warts and all, and accepts us just as we are. We need a person in this world with whom it is safe to be ourselves. A person who is safe to know and to be known by. A person we can love and who will show us love. To understand and to be understood. It can be a spouse, it can be a friend, it can be anyone, you just need your person. A person or persons to be connected with. Your soul is unique, no one else on earth is just like you. That soul needs to be known and expressed and accepted.

Third, we need purpose. We need a reason to get up in the mornings, a reason to continue to grow, a reason to keep moving forward. When the ground is shaking when the water is overwhelming, when the walls are crumbling, when the chaos is coming at us, we need a reason to keep moving forward. Purpose provides that.

Now, here is where I am going to talk a little more about that connection with God. It intersects with our purpose. I want to look at a scripture in Mark 6. Jesus and the disciples had just fed the 5,000 and following that we have these words:

[45] Immediately he made his disciples get into

the boat and go on ahead to the other side, to Bethsaida, while he dismissed the crowd. [46] After saying farewell to them, he went up on the mountain to pray.

[47] When *evening* came, the boat was out on the sea, and he was alone on the land. [48] When he saw that they were straining at the oars against an adverse wind, he came towards them *early in the morning,* walking on the sea. *He intended to pass them by.* [49] But when they saw him walking on the sea, they thought it was a ghost and cried out; [50] for they all saw him and were terrified. But immediately he spoke to them and said, "Take heart, it is I; do not be afraid."

Jesus didn't go to them immediately; hours had passed. Walking on the sea, he intended to pass them by. I hadn't caught that before when I had read this. Had you caught that before? He was standing on land, he was praying, he knew about the storm, hours had passed by and some translations say until the fourth watch, which tells us exactly when in the morning. So, hours had passed by before Jesus, knowing about the storm and the conditions his disciples were facing, went out to them. And he intended to *pass them by*!!!

How many times, when you have been in your metaphorical boat, in the middle of a storm, has your soul cried out for Jesus to come and jump in that boat and be present with you powerfully right there, right then? This passage tells us that Jesus doesn't have to be right there, right then. Jesus is aware of the storm. Even when he is up on the mountain praying, he knows that his people are out, struggling against an adverse wind. He also knows it is enough to simply pass by. He knows it doesn't have to happen immediately.

Why would Jesus wait?

What do you think happened in the hearts and minds and souls of those disciples in those hours before Jesus went out on the water? They struggled.

If I were in that situation, the first thing I would have done would be to panic. Then, my better angels would have kicked in and said, "Ok, now take a breath and calm down and try to figure out what to do to survive." These thoughts come in nanoseconds and you evaluate what you have, evaluate what you need and how you can get through from one second to the next. You are ter-rified, and you have to summon the courage, and you have this on-going film reel in the back of your head of what is really important in your life and what is vital.

Ultimately you realize that the only place to cry out for help is to that which transcends all things. That is an important part of being human. When we are raising children, we don't follow them around and keep them from falling (after the first one). We try to tell them things that are good to know and to follow, but let's face it, it is usu-ally a waste of breath, and they have to figure it out for themselves. They have to go through that process of learning where their boundaries are and where their gifts are, what they can do and what they can't do and what it is to panic and what it is to calm themselves down; how to find courage within themselves. Children have to go through those things, just as every adult does. Everyone who has breath and life, follows that journey. We need that and during those times, the connection to God grows stronger and our purpose grows ever clearer.

When that purpose grows within us and

springs forth from the solid ground upon which we live and breathe and have our being, our spirits grow and develop; and like sunflowers with their face to the sun, grow ever closer to God.

I will be forever thankful that God gives me what I need, rather than what I want. I'm not very good at seeking what I need over what I want. Thank you, Jesus, for teaching me to pray about that.

## For Further Reflection

1. How do you distinguish between wants and needs?
2. What have you given up as unnecessary that you used to cling to?
3. What or whom do you lean on or depend upon? What helps you to orient yourself in this life?
4. How have these things proven to be insufficient?
5. What internal shift do you need to make in order for God to be your true foundation?
6. How will this internal shift manifest itself in

your daily life? In your priorities? In your activities?

7. How has God revealed to you your purpose? What do you need in order to find this within yourself?

8. How does your purpose intersect with your community's needs?

9. How do you see yourself growing in this capacity?

5
———

# I Have To What?

*Forgive us our sins, as we forgive those who sin against us.*

One might say that this is the hardest work of faith. Let's begin our discussion on this with a powerful story, one that you are probably familiar with, Corrie Ten Boom. She was a Hollander and sheltered Jews in her home during the Nazi invasion and was caught and imprisoned, due to a clerical error, during World War II. Corrie Ten Boom was released from Ravensbruck Concentration Camp one week before all the women her age were killed. She began traveling and telling the story of her family and what she and her sister, Betsy, had learned there. She recounts one story in particular.

Ten Boom was speaking at a church in Munich about how God forgives. To her chagrin, a man came up to her afterwards whom she immediately recognized as a guard at Ravensbruck, where she and her sister had been sent. Her sister did not survive her time there.

He told her that he had a conversion after his time there and had come to follow Christ. He told Corrie that he knew God had forgiven him, but he wanted her forgiveness as well. He reached his hand out to her.

She described those next moments thusly:

"I stood there, I am one whose sins had every day been forgiven and Betsy had died in that place, a slow and terrible death. Could it be forgiven just simply by asking?

It could not have been many seconds that he stood there with his hand held out to me, but it seemed hours as I wrestled with the most difficult thing I ever had to do. I had to do it, I knew the message that God forgives has a prior condition, that we forgive those who have injured us.

If you do not forgive them in their trespasses, Jesus says neither will your Father in heaven forgive you your trespasses.

I stood there with the coldness clutching in my heart, but forgiveness is not an emotion. I knew that to forgive is an act of the will and the world can function regardless of the temperature of the heart. "Jesus, help me," I prayed silently. I can lift my hand. I can do that much. You supply the rest.

So, weirdly, mechanically, I thrust my hand into the one stretched out to me. As I did an incredible thing took place. The current started in my shoulder. It raced down my arm and sprang into our joint hands and then, this healing work seemed to flood my whole being, bringing tears to my eyes.

I forgive you brother, I cried with all my heart. For a long moment we grasped each other's hands, the former guard, the former prisoner. I have never known God's love as intensely as I did then."

*I have never known God's love as intensely as I did then.*

Can you imagine?

Let's talk about this for a minute. First let's talk about the guard. He knew God had forgiven him, and he listened to Corrie Ten Boom talk about forgiveness: God's forgiveness. Now he had received forgiveness from her. There's still another person who needs to supply forgiveness for him and that's going to be the hardest one yet. Who do you think that is?

That would be himself. Ten Boom forgave him but he still has to live with the knowledge of all that he willfully did to other people. Even knowing that God forgives him, even knowing that Corrie forgives him, he still lives every day with that knowledge and struggles with that.

Is it fair to say that when Corrie forgave him, he was off the hook? If he has had a conversion moment, then he wrestles with that. Forgiveness is not a get out of jail free card. It is not an "OK check you're no longer responsible, it's all OK, box and move on" moment. He will wrestle with his past actions for the rest of his life.

What is forgiveness?

Let's talk about what happened within Ten Boom in that moment. Did she want to forgive this man? No! She knew she should though; it was incumbent by her faith to do so, but if she could have an out – she wanted an out. She did it, not by her own strength, but by God's strength. The result? She felt the love of God in a way she never had before that moment. She experienced liberation in that moment.

A part of me wonders what she would say to us today if she were here and able to answer questions. I don't want to put words in her mouth, but if we asked her if she had not forgiven him, what life would be like for her, I wouldn't be surprised if she said that she felt imprisoned in a way that she was kind of stuck in, that in that time she was unable to move beyond it, still stuck with what happened in that camp. When she forgave him, she did not say, 'OK it's over, none of it matters any longer.' What she was saying by forgiving him is, 'that event and what you did is no longer going to imprison me. I'm going to free myself from this.'

If you ever want to keep somebody close to you, resent them. They are with you all of the time. They are going to be on your mind when you wake up in the morning. They are going to be on your mind when you try to sleep at night, and when you wake up at 1 o'clock, 2 o'clock, 3o'clock, 4 o'clock, and 5 o'clock in the morning. Whenever you sit down to eat, they're going to disrupt your digestion. The surest way to keep somebody close to you is to bear resentment for them. Forgiveness removes that person and that resentment from holding you hostage to a bad experience.

When Ten Boom forgave this man, she said 'I'm letting you go so I can be free.' That is a powerful, powerful thing to experience. Forgiving others is the hardest work of faith, because we just don't wanna! I never feel like a toddler more than when I'm wrestling with myself over forgiving someone, because, doggone it, I just don't wanna! (Be assured that my upper lip is stuck out, and my arms are crossed in front of me.)

I can't do that work on my own. It all starts with God.

Help me here. I was wrestling with the sentence: 'forgive us our sins *AS* we forgive those who sin against us.' That two-letter word – as. What does that word mean in this sentence? Does it mean 'in the amount of time?' In other words, are we saying, hey there, God, as I'm praying and asking for your forgiveness, please take this same amount of time to also forgive me and forgive others that have sinned against me? That's a pretty short window! It takes 20 seconds to say the Lord's prayer, so this one word in this one line within that 20 seconds is maybe one second. Let's be generous and give it three seconds, then if we interpret the word 'as', in an amount of time that passes while speaking; that's still not much time.

What do you think about looking at this word, 'as,' to mean 'in the manner of?' God, forgive me my sins 'in the same manner' that I forgive those who sin against me. Now, I have created a problem for myself, because I'm right back to I don't wanna!! I've set up a standard by which I'm going to be forgiven. I'm asking God to forgive me to the same extent and in the same way I have forgiven others. I don't think God works that way. I don't think we can put limits on, or set free, what God does or what God wills or what God wants. I think we push past that a little further.

That two-letter (I'm beginning to feel like it's a four-letter) word, 'as.'

Forgive us *as* we forgive.

Perhaps it's an acknowledgement of understanding. Forgive us as we have been forgiven. It's an acknowledgement that this is God's business. This is God's work; this is Godly action. God is all about doing this, and it's not on the merit system, it's because it's in the nature of God to forgive. God forgives us because that's who God is and what God chooses to do. Therefore, acknowledging that God is a forgiving God, allows me to participate in what God *is doing* in this world. I want to join in what God is doing. I want to be a part of that work. I want to be a part of this kingdom. So: "God - as you have forgiven, forgive me too, and help me to forgive others. I want in."

This Lord's Prayer, it's really tricky, isn't it?

We say it often and we say it so much that it's a part of who we are. I think it's in the fiber of our being. If our memory were wiped clean and somebody came in and said the Lord's Prayer, I think that it's so deeply within us that we would be able to say it right along with the other person. It becomes a part of us.

And yet, when we take the time to really look at what's going on here, it's a little frightening, to be honest with you, because I really believe that God answers prayer – especially if we pray the way that GOD INCARNATE has told us to pray!

When we pray the Lord's Prayer, we begin with: what are we going to call God – how do we understand God and then acknowledge God's holiness?

After that we pray for God's kingdom to come to earth as it is in heaven. That's going to mess up a lot of stuff for us that we like, because many of us benefit from the inequity in our world. God's really stepping on our toes, there. (Deep sigh) But we pray that anyway, because we trust that God will be God and, ultimately, it's going to be best for us. It's going to be uncomfortable for a time, but it'll be ok. Better than ok, because when all people are recognized as God's precious and chosen people, we all benefit. But until then, as long as some of us are diminished, none of us can realize our true worth and potential.

Then, give us what we need, God, not really what we want but what we need.

Forgive us our sins as we forgive those who sin against us.

The Lord's prayer is heavy business, but it is Godly business.

If you want to be a part of what God is doing in this world and you pray for God to come to you and make this work a reality in this life, and you ask God for what you need and then you seek to do this hardest work – that's a powerful model of prayer! We're not even finished praying yet, and already the world (me) transforms.

Have you known anyone who has forgiven something greater than you could think about? I do. I had a conversation with a woman who said if she had not forgiven him (her offender), she would've been trapped. When she said goodbye and forgave him, she was finally free of him, and free to be her own person. What happened would no longer define her.

Forgiveness.

Sometimes it's easy. If you accidentally bump into somebody and say I'm sorry, forgiveness isn't so difficult. It's a little bit different than when there's been an act of violence or an act that has changed a person, or one's family. It is the hardest work of faith.

It's also the most transformative work of faith. Forgiving one's self is the key that unlocks our growth spiritually and emotionally. We all have that thing (or maybe things) about ourselves that we don't ever want others to know about us. We don't like to think about it. When we do we feel all sorts of icky feelings. Allowing light to shine through that darkness within us frees us. Chances are, that thing is a manifestation of our soul's deepest need, and its attempt to fill it. Learning how to identify that and to forgive that little girl or little boy inside us does some kind of miracle that changes us. We become more patient. More tolerant. More understanding. More loving. We simply become more.

So, do it. Just do it. Do it, because it's hard to do. Because it's important to do. Do it, because you seek in this life what God can offer. Do it because you can't do it by yourself and it will bring you closer to the love of God than you've ever been before.

And then take it a step further. Forgive others. Your friends. Your family. Your neighbors. People you don't like… People you would like to hate because their differences are too much to stomach. Our world is so divided, so polarized. We live on a hair trigger, firing at the slightest provocation. We live with hatred for people of different skin tones and sexual orientation, Biblical interpretation, political beliefs, and so many other things. Even though we don't want to harbor these feelings, they are so deeply ingrained in the daily business of living in this day and time that we are a part of it. In this cancel-culture world we live in, we would rather defeat and silence those who are different than us than to understand them.

*Forgive us our sins as we forgive those who sin against us.*

It's quite possible (probable?) that forgiveness extends beyond the person-person, to a societal level. What would it look like for a society to take an honest and hard look at itself, confess its sins, and forgive itself; and then reach outward and, as a society, forgive those it has wronged? Is this even possible?

It is. With God.

I don't know how to start, but I do believe that the Lord's Prayer, this ancient model that Jesus shared with his disciples, calls us to do this work. Any human institution will inherently be corrupt. Even those human institutions that find their identities in the love and grace of God. Maybe especially those. So how can we not engage in this communal work? How do we start?

I don't have the answer to this question, but I believe it's a plane we can build as we fly. It begins within each of us. If we begin with the difficult and very personal work of forgiving ourselves, God will lead us to the next step. This is a pretty big project when we step back and look at it; daunting even. We need God to do the heavy lifting. If you can't forgive, or even bring yourself to want to forgive, talk to God about it. And go from there. Even if you throw a fit or two. Or twenty. Or seventy times seven.

## For Further Reflection

1. For what have you been forgiven, that you still struggle to overcome within yourself?
2. What feelings come up inside you when you hear about forgiveness? What do these feelings mean to you?
3. Who do you resent? Who is that person that you do not like to hear good news of? How is this person stealing your joy in life?
4. What do you want regarding this person? How can you begin to get to a place where you can ask God to help you forgive? What do you need?
5. How would your life be different once this is accomplished?

6. With whom could you have a conversation about forgiveness on a broader level? What would be the topic? To whom would you offer a confession and apology? How could this bring about greater freedom for you?

6

———

# Worrying Above My Paygrade

*Lead us not into temptation, but deliver us from evil*

*I put this final sermon together for Sunday, July 5<sup>th</sup>, 2020; in the middle of a pandemic, of a time of reckoning regarding race relations, and a hostile political atmosphere. Each day seemed to bring more bad news. Rates of addiction and suicide were escalating. People were angry all the time. Tolerance for others was very low. We were just beginning (where we lived) to come out of quarantine and be around other people (at a dis-*

*tance). In the middle of all of this, comes a word of hope. Whatever context you are in as you read this, I hope you find a word of hope as well.*

We celebrate Independence Day this weekend, and as so many others have noted, there were so many fireworks! More than I ever recall. I think we needed something to celebrate. We weren't able to get together and have corned beef and cabbage on St. Patrick's Day. We didn't get to eat a bunch of tacos together on Cinco de Mayo. But, doggone it, on July Fourth we will have our grilled meat and the fireworks, and all that goes with it. Our family went to a local village's fireworks display on Friday night. And last night (on the 4th) all we had to do was step outside. We could see fireworks in all directions. It was fun! It felt good. It felt good to see other people. It felt good to celebrate. It felt good to once again declare independence from the tyranny of living in a pandemic.

I realized, as I was taking all this in, that if one wants to be truly independent, one needs a strong and firm foundation upon which to stand. We need to know who we are and Whose we are, or we will be blown about by every wind that blows our way. If you have a firm foundation and understanding of who you are in relation to all else, you are able to withstand the ill winds. God is the only foundation I know of that will not crumble beneath my feet. To be independent, is to be firmly rooted in God, particularly, as Christians, the way we have come to know God in Jesus Christ. Ironically, the more dependent we are upon God, the more independent we are in the world.

A way we root ourselves deeply in our faith is through prayer. Especially paying attention to the methods that Jesus (God Incarnate) has taught us.

1. How do we address God and acknowledge God's holiness? Who God is, defines who we are.
2. Pray that God's deepest and greatest expectations come to be a reality right now in our lives that we all can live and breathe and have our being.
3. Pray for what we need, remembering that God is neither Santa Claus nor Amazon.
4. Pray that we are gracious and forgiving people, because that's how we jump into the work that God's doing.

And now we come to the last: *lead us not into temptation but deliver us from evil.*

As I look around, I see so many of us succumbing to the temptation of anger. It feels like the river of grace and understanding we were accustomed to has dried up, and we are left with nothing to extend to our neighbors, nothing other than our judgment and anger. Our tolerance of different opinions and choices has all but disappeared, and it's taking its toll on all of us. We're doing a lot of talking AT each other instead of to and with each other. This leads to a lack of listening. And hearing. And understanding. It sure feels like everybody is shouting their views all the time and telling others how stupid they are for their own. I'm not exaggerating. Social media only magnifies this effect. We get so caught up in this rancor, to the point of distraction. When good and godly people are caught up in their own stuff and correcting others' stuff – guess what can flourish?

Evil.

Evil has a field day when we are distracted and not paying attention. So, to be independent and celebrate freedom, it's important to be grounded on a solid and firm foundation, so we're not reacting to every wind that blows counter to us. If we react to all the stuff, not only are we distracted, but we often find ourselves fussing and arguing. There are absolutely occasions for righteous anger – without a doubt – but, if we make our home on that fleeting territory, it's easy to stumble. And evil abounds. 'Cause we're tired. 'Cause we've used all our energy on other things. What does it say about us if we fight passionately for life in every corner of our world, and never notice the signs of death in our own homes? What does it say about us if we tirelessly fight to correct the ills of our society, and have nothing left for the people we see everyday?

Temptation, in its many and varied forms, always seeks to have us lose ourselves in something that destroys. Whether that temptation comes in the form of food, drink, drugs, gambling, sex, arguing, slander, or any other form – it seeks to draw us in until we lose ourselves, lose ourselves in something that destroys.

*Lead us not into temptation, O God!! Deliver us from evil.*

I've been in ministry more than twenty years now. There are two things about people I have learned. The first is this: we don't like change, and the second one is similar: we don't like uncertainty. Change and uncertainty are two things that humans, by and large, do not handle well. Guess what this pandemic and all the other things that have accompanied it have brought to us? Change. Uncertainty. Even if we're living good lives and going about our business, we were thrust into change and uncertainty. Want to plan for the annual family get-together? Good luck. Did you have a wedding with a hundred guests invited? Sorry. Were you looking forward to finally seeing your favorite band in concert? Too bad. Waiting for school to start in the fall? Don't plan on it. We don't know what the rules will be tomorrow. We can make the best decisions we can, based on the best information we have, but it could all change tomorrow. Throw in some natural and human made disasters, rough political times, and some existential threats and it's difficult to imagine regaining solid ground again.

In these circumstances, evil abounds. It flourishes. It destroys.

We need a way to inoculate our faith against it all. So, we pray, "lead us not into temptation, deliver us from evil." There are some actions we can take to facilitate this.

First, is to breathe. Stop what you're doing and take a breath. Take another. Relax and take a few more. Make sure that you are living in the moment and not bringing in unneeded anxiety and worry. A friend of mine, who was caring for a parent, was helping her mother do this exact thing. Her mother had been taking a lot of medications for a long time and the doctors were trying to reduce the amount she was taking to uncover what she really needed medically. One of the medications being withdrawn managed anxiety. This was proving difficult. Her mother felt anxious all the time.

"Mom, why are you anxious?" Mom replied, "because of everything going on right now!" "Mom," she asked again, "why are you anxious?" "Everything seems like it's coming apart at the seams – the world is a mess!" "Mom," she said, "You have a home that is paid for. You have air conditioning to keep you comfortable in the heat of summer and a furnace to keep you warm in winter. Your food is prepared for you. Your family loves you and surrounds you. All you need to do is your laundry, and you have what you need to do that. Why are you anxious?"

Her mother's anxiety didn't disappear, but it was put into perspective and she was better able to manage it. The mother realized that she was listening to a lot of loud voices, and she had allowed those voices to have authority over her. By stopping, breathing, and deciding to live in the moment, she was better able to go about her day and be attentive to the things important to her.

What a powerful awareness! There are SO MANY loud voices shouting at us in the best of times – let alone when we are vulnerable. What voices are you giving authority to? Do these voices build you up or tear you down? Pay attention to what you are paying attention to. When you feel the weight of stress and anxiety, stop and breathe. Look around you. How much of what you are worried about is an actual reality right now? The things that have you so stressed – are they actually real and tangible right now, or are they only possibilities that may develop? If they are voices that don't deserve the authority you are giving them – revoke that authority. Tune them out and put your mind on Jesus.

Which is the second step in our inoculation. Get your mind on Jesus. Every night when we sleep, there are glial cells in our brains that clean out the garbage. These glial cells are like little Roomba vacuums. They go about their business, and whatever isn't fastened down is swept away. Thoughts, facts, ideas, beliefs; these things get fastened down in our brain through neural pathways that are created. And how are these neural pathways created, you ask? (Thank you for asking!) The more time we spend thinking on something, the more neural pathways are formed. Think about that. (See what I did there?) Our brains classify something as important when we spend time thinking about it. Which begs the question: what do you spend your time thinking about? Whatever the answer to that is, is what your reality will be.

So…what do you spend time thinking about? What you feed your mind nourishes your soul. Are you getting the recommended daily allowances of "soul" food? I often discover that when I am in a rut or going through a time of drudgery, it is also true that I have spent time filling my brain with thoughts and entertainment that don't feed my soul. It's fun to watch a silly movie or read a superfluous magazine. Do you spend time thinking about people and situations that make you angry, or time thinking how you can bring reconciliation? Be mindful that you are spending time filling your thoughts with what is truly important and lasting. In so doing, we more firmly root ourselves on solid ground. The more you keep your mind on Jesus – the more Jesus will shape and form you.

Take a breath, get your mind on Jesus, and then cut yourself a little slack. You may be a little resistant to this next bit but hear me out. Go and get a tattoo on your forehead that says, "I'm not in charge of the world." Get it put on backwards, so that every time you look in a mirror you will see it. You are not in charge of the world. I'm not in charge of the world. The world will continue with or without us. It's important to remember that there are some things beyond our control. When we spend time worrying about things we cannot control, we are worrying above our pay grade. Stop it. (I saw you roll your eyes.)

I have to remind myself of that from time to time. On Sunday mornings I connect cameras and iPads on our network in order to record and broadcast our Sunday services. I have a routine that I go through to ensure that all the details are managed. Some days I find myself stressing out over our internet's upload speed. I have to remind myself that I have done all the things I can do to maintain our network. What happens beyond that is out of my control. I don't need to expend time and energy worrying above my paygrade.

I know some folks who have raised worrying to an art form. They worry that they're not worrying about all things that need worrying about. You know who you are. If this is you, start developing a new habit. Start with five minutes each day thinking through how things will go well. Then increase the time. Don't give into the temptation to worry without spending time imagining a good outcome.

Take a breath. Get your mind on Jesus. Tattoo your forehead (or find an equally effective way) so you remember to take time and intentional action to sort out what you can control and what you cannot. If you can control it, act on it. If you cannot, don't worry above your pay grade. Do what you have the power to do.

Paul said (Philippians 2:12) to work out our

own salvation with fear and trembling. I think this is what he was talking about. The end of the Lord's Prayer (as recorded in Matthew) is all about deliverance and salvation. *Lead us not into temptation but deliver us from evil.* Turning from temptation into deliverance – what a powerful request! Some two thousand years ago, Jesus showed us the depth of love God has for us, in that NOTHING would separate us from the love of God. Our eternal salvation is accomplished. What's at stake for us today is deliverance from all that would bind us and blind us to the depth and breadth of God's love. Take a breath. Get your mind on Jesus. Do what you have the power to do. God is God, and we are not. That's solid ground. That's something to build upon.

## For Further Reflection

1. Are you a worrier? What are the things you worry about that you have no direct control over? How would it feel to set these aside?
2. What do you spend time thinking about

throughout the day? Are these the things you want 'hardwired' in your brain?

3. How would it help you to spend 10 minutes each evening reviewing your day, and focusing on what was important to you?

4. What habits do you need to let go of? What thoughts and activities are putting barriers between you and God and the life you want?

# 7

## Conclusion

I was hiking once and came across a rocky crag that had a tree bursting through, demanding to be acknowledged. It grew sideways out of the rock and then took a ninety-degree turn upward, growing toward the light. What a marvel. As a biologist, I can tell you the biochemical processes behind this growth. But I would rather tell you, as a beloved daughter of God, that we can pass through rocky places and grow toward the light.

When light shines, it activates something deep down inside of us, nurturing, feeding, beckoning. What feels better after the depths of winter than emerging into the sunshine and turning our face to the light? We can feel life stirring within us, awaking to the new possibilities the light brings.

If you have a houseplant by a window, you know you have to turn it periodically, because it grows toward the light. If you've endeavored to grow your spirit, you also know that it will orient itself to The Light. After doing a deep dive into the Lord's Prayer, I have come to see that Jesus gives us a model of prayer that enables The Light to reach our depths.

Opening our eyes to the manifold ways God is present to us, seeking to be transformed by God to do the work of God, finding contentment in our met needs, forgiving and releasing anger and bitterness, and keeping our hearts and minds on what is holy – these things remove any obstacles that block The Light from reaching us down to our roots. Adopting this model of prayer and leaning into it regularly is life-giving. We read again and again how Jesus withdrew and prayed, and how it lifted him to a holy place, filled to overflowing with the love, grace, and mercy of God.

I've seen how praying the words of the model itself crawls deeply into our very bones; in Christ I see how leaning into this model of prayer is transformational. As a traveler on this road myself, my prayer is for you to turn to The Light and feel the life within you waking to what God has for you. For to God is the glory and the power for ever and ever. Amen.

Melissa was called into ministry, much to her surprise, after becoming a biologist and serving for ten years in the IL Army National Guard as a utility helicopter mechanic, the first woman to do so.

Having lived in the Midwest, Melissa has a deep appreciation for farmers and the lessons of the Gospel dramatized by the sowing, tending, and harvesting year after year.

*"God's glory and God's story are all around us if we take the time to see. Lessons of life and death, struggle and celebration, heartbreak and harvest - life always wins."*

Melissa's passion in ministry is to live and worship alongside the people who live and work in rural communities. She has served the Illiopolis Christian Church (DOC) since July 2, 2001. January 1, 2012 Melissa began serving both Illiopolis and Niantic Christian Churches (DOC) and continues in ministry there today.

Melissa is at home in the difficult spaces of peoples' lives, willing to listen and to walk with those who struggle and suffer. She is a trained coach and has consulted with churches in conflict. Not your stereotypical minister, Melissa embraces the Gospel with joy and laughter as she seeks to help those around her grow in faith and understanding, always striving to leave people better than they came. An agent of wholeness, Melissa works to invite others into a space where they can understand how ridiculously loved and valued they are by a God who also may not fit a stereotype.

To learn more about Light Life and Love Ministries, and to work with Melissa, go to www.lightlifeandloveministries.com. Join the community to grow your faith!

**Melissa Ebken, Light Life and Love Ministries**

www.ingramcontent.com/pod-product-compliance
Lightning Source LLC
Chambersburg PA
CBHW061043050726
47592CB00004B/1566